HOW TO MANAGE YOUR OFFICE WORKER LIKE A FRIENDLY BOSS

2

Contents

3

Even after the employee goes, stay in contact 45

INTRODUCTION

How do you manage people?

The process of organizing, managing, and developing the employee side of a firm is known as people management. Supporting a full team's work as well as their wellbeing, engagement, and progress are all responsibilities of management jobs.

Making sure that everyone feels heard, understood, cared for, and given the resources they need to succeed—while also attempting to ensure that they are succeeding in accordance with company metrics—requires more than just creating tasks and assigning them, according to Tile.

That is a rather difficult request, particularly for those with several direct reports. Weekly one-on-ones, team meetings, and going through each team member's weekly report soon add up. Additionally, it may be particularly difficult to strike a balance between your personal requirements and those of your team when you are a team player. Examples of such demands include concentrate time, organization, and professional development.

Here are seven suggestions for new managers, including where to get help, how to cultivate positive attitudes, and how to lead with compassion.

Some individuals are pushed into management while others are born to it. Choosing the kind of manager you want to be in your new position is one of the first stages, regardless of the route you choose to setting up weekly one-on-ones.

"As a rookie manager, you want to avoid becoming a people-pleaser. In addition, you are trying not to be rigid, stated Piranha Tile, Lead Producer at City Cast DC. "I am attempting to make sure that everyone I report to is pleased, as well as all of my direct reports. Because I am concentrating on everyone else, sometimes I feel like my needs are neglected. The process of making sure the correct people are in the right position, with the proper resources, to accomplish the intended objectives is known as people management. This covers hiring, educating, and fostering the growth of your team members.

Throughout their whole careers, employees' experiences are greatly influenced by management. Employee performance and retention are significantly impacted by management attitudes and practices, particularly when dealing with change.

People management and leadership have a lot in common, and effective managers also become effective leaders. There are some significant changes, however. Managers are often more concerned with day-to-day operations, while leaders frequently play a more strategic role.

It might be challenging to find a competent people manager with the right traits. Everyone wants to follow a competent, assured, and resolute leader.

How do you approach that individual, though? What are the requirements for maintaining that position? What if you are just getting started and have little prior management experience?

Many of my students are aspiring managers of people or have just begun having people report to them. Most of the time, these individuals really care about their staff and are eager to learn how to best serve them.

In the beginning, what counts most is the sincerity of their treatment. From there, we build abilities and knowledge to become really powerful, encouraging, and sympathetic people managers.

Finding that balance may be difficult, counterintuitive, and perplexing. Even exceptional managers require help and structure to succeed; although managing abilities do often take time to perfect, they also do not miraculously emerge on their own. Developing your management abilities is crucial for showcasing potential at work and assisting your team in reaching its objectives. It may be difficult to ensure that everyone onboard a project works well together as a team and effectively completes duties, but there are a number of tried-and-true methods you can use to enhance your management skills while working with others.

In this essay, we outline the qualities of a successful manager and provide thorough guidelines for leading and managing your team to success.

Any manager has to have the ability to manage people. No matter how long you have been in the position or how new it is, developing this ability will increase employee engagement and productivity.

However, a competent manager may make a difficult job bearable. A poor management can destroy a good job.

When I reflect on my own career, a few important people managers jump out as exceptional and a few that I would avoid if I encountered them in a job interview.

The ones that stick out are the ones who, in the opinion of my colleagues and myself, actually cared about what we wanted and the success of our company.

These are the supervisors who never made me feel incapable. Instead, they pushed me to give it a go and take something away from the experience.

After 15 years of management experience in a variety of settings and job responsibilities, I now share these positive lessons with aspiring and seasoned leaders via graduate-level courses at the Pamplona School of Business at the University of Portland.

In this article, we will go over the fundamentals of people management, a few different people management approaches, and what you can do to start on the path to being a successful people manager.

Great leadership seems to be a simple task since it lacks any super-secret methods. But although while outstanding leadership often consists of straightforward actions, for some reason, many leaders neglect to put them into practice.

The following leadership advice is, of course, merely the tip of the iceberg. Like everything else in life, actual practice is required in this situation since theory alone is insufficient.

- A comprehensive approach to assisting workers' work, development, and well-being is people management.
- In management positions, you must strike a balance between providing your own work and helping others.
- Managers should utilize direct report feedback to determine how they can grow as leaders.
- Courses, mentors, and fellow managers may all serve as sources of inspiration for managers.

1. Prioritize managing your own workload.

You must take care of yourself first before you can manage the success of others. Protect your time and prioritize your calendar by blocking out a period of time each day to focus only on doing your own job without distractions. Over committing to their team is a mistake that eager managers may make, which leads to burnout and reduces their management effectiveness. You will be more attentive and focused on your team when they need you if you are comfortable with your own job.

Direct management of individuals

The manager instructs staff members on what and how to do tasks. This management style works best when activities need to be accomplished fast and effectively in accordance with a specified standard or need, but it may also put staff under a lot of stress.

Additionally, it works best for workers who are still developing as well as in societies or situations where people must be informed explicitly what to do, how to do it, and when.

Fun fact: Micromanagement does not demonstrate to a worker your concern for their job.

Micromanaging an employee shows that you do not have faith in them to do high-quality job on their own.

Working with an employee to solve an issue collaboratively is far different from micromanaging them while they tackle their own problems.

Be kind.

Never lose sight of the fact that the actual people you are managing have genuine problems and real experiences. For many business executives, employees are only man-hours that need to be controlled and maximized.

Regardless of whether they are your people, friends, or man-hours, your team always understands who they are for you. Additionally, a man-hour will not ever solve your problems.

Acquire management skills

Few of us naturally have the ability to lead others, and I have not come across any "leadership courses" that are really valuable. Thankfully, we have something far better at our disposal in the form of books. You will have to stand up for your organization's interests as a leader. And you will fare much better if you comprehend the other person's mind and are familiar with negotiating philosophy.

A leader must thus read literature. Leaders should study about psychology, the way the mind works, recruiting, negotiating, marketing, project management, and economics in addition to management.

Find out who is who.

Know yourself and the people on your team. You can achieve this with the aid of my four playground characters. "What kind of kid was I on the playground?" you could ask. The person who

- Ensured that everyone had a chance to bat? The mediator.
- Created a line, then had everyone count off? The coordinator.
- Halfway through the game, the rules were changed? An innovator.
- Wanted to approach it in my way? The sledgehammer.

Decide who is on your playground once you have determined your playground personality. Do not ignore the warnings. Body language, word choice, and intentions are all quite evident in human interaction.

Collaboration and communication are important to peacemakers. When others fight, a staff member's eyes may swell, which is a red flag.

Organizers are methodical and determined. An employee is an organizer if he shows up to a meeting with charts or paper that is color-coded.

Revolutionaries despise regularity and favor improvisation. A revolutionary will be evident if you question, "Where did that come from?"

Having strong opinions and the intelligence to tackle challenging issues, steamrollers. They adopt conflicting points of view and maintain concepts at 30,000 feet.

Spend time discovering the distinctive qualities of your staff. Everyone offers their own special skills to the team, such as how they respond to criticism the best, whether they get up early, and their multitasking prowess. Spend some time getting to know each one; it will enable you to put a face on them and better comprehend how they function.

According to Kelly Moon, director of content at Send Bird, "I share a getting-to-know-you worksheet where we know about each other's communication style and what motivates and inspires us." Since everyone is unique, "I tailor my management style to each individual."

Understanding the requirements of your employees will help you understand their actions, inclinations, and difficulties at work. Even when working with distant teams, this subtlety may help you more effectively convey performance goals and resolve issues.

When it comes to communication, Moon advised being "really communicative right out of the gate so that people do not feel confused about what to expect." He also recommended enabling opportunities for team members to get to know one another better. Establishing a strong team connection helps everyone feel committed to the objective and stay resilient in the face of change or uncertainty. Therefore, it is important to provide chances for the team to spend time together and develop trust with one another.

Assign tasks

Instead of supervising each work on a project, you may concentrate on high-level management responsibilities by learning how to delegate important tasks to others. You will be able to assign tasks to those who are most likely to complete them efficiently and within the allotted time limit after you have a better understanding of each team member's strengths, weaknesses, experiences, and talents. When assigning duties, it is important to establish clear expectations with each employee and make sure they have faith in their capacity to do their assigned share of the project. You may show people that you have faith in their skills by assigning them tasks, which will make them feel engaged in the success of the project.

People management coaching

The manager assists staff in obtaining the required results by giving them clear, detailed instructions. This management approach works well to teach individuals certain habits and cultural norms so that the boss may eventually be less directive and more supportive.

When highly capable people are transitioning to a new company culture or situation, the coaching approach is useful in helping them adopt certain habits.

Recognize the situation you are in

Expertise is the only way to gain authority. All leaders, regardless of their position, must have a thorough understanding of the items they oversee.

For instance, you need to be quite knowledgeable about the tools, APIs, arrays, functions, and algorithm complexity if you want to head a development team. Ideally, you ought to have worked as a developer in the past. It is understandable why Mark Zuckerberg and Sergey Bring were so successful at operating IT businesses given that they could communicate with customers in their own language.

Even if your team employs many programming languages and you do not fully understand all of their intricacies, you should be able to comprehend their code and be aware of the major frameworks.

You will not be in a position to accurately evaluate the timeliness, risks, or costs unless you have a solid grasp of what you manage.

Be respectful. Respect begins with the boss. Hello and thank you are important greetings. To be respectful:

Together with peacemakers, generate ideas.

Give the organizers work that has deadlines and is important.

Give revolutionaries urgent jobs to do.

Ask the views of steamrollers.

Admit reality. Ask questions, be willing to learn, and avoid cutting off dialogues too soon since not everyone gathers information in the same manner that you do. When you believe you have all the information, confirm by asking again.

Encourage mentoring partnerships

You should try to establish a mentorship connection with your staff if you want to improve as a manager. Making long-term development goals, offering professional counsel and direction, and assisting your staff in recognizing career advancement prospects are all part of being an effective mentor.

Strong decision-making abilities must be shown.

Whenever there is a dispute or a decision to be made about the workplace, managers often have the last say. Making unbiased choices, regardless of the team members involved, should be one of your goals as you strive to become a better manager.

Encouraging teamwork

An effective manager is conscious of the fact that his or her success depends on the cooperation of the team. You need do more than just make sure your team functions as a unit to improve as a manager. You should work to enhance the standing of your team inside the organization. Using unbiased techniques to assess team members' performance and resolving any conflicts that may emerge should be part of your team development activities.

Utilize 1:1s for development and strategic problem-solving.
Although it may be tempting, face-to-face time is best spent for important discussions rather than serving as a checklist for ongoing tasks.

"One-on-ones give us the space to talk about the big picture, like how our production process is working or not, and how we might want to revamp it," said Tile. "The weekly one-on-one would become bogged down in that stuff if we were not doing the small things on a daily basis."

Spend your synchronous time more carefully, particularly if you have more than one direct report, as long as you have other ways to communicate project statuses (such

Lattice Weekly Updates and Slack, or project management platforms like Jeri, Asana, or Trellis).

In those one-on-one sessions, Tilde said, "we identify problems that people are experiencing (particularly around impending burnout) and then find ways to either mitigate that or prevent it from becoming a problem in the first place." "Watching those solutions materialize has been really satisfying."

Make sure you take the time to discuss collectively bigger patterns that emerge in your workflow and team members' career aspirations. "How can I support them? What were the successes, what worked or did not work?" Lunar said. Then they have a secure environment where they feel free to be open and honest, and we can work through problems together.

You may organize your weekly chats using the agenda form from our one-on-one meetings.

Control the conversation

Take the initiative when talking with others by asking questions, seeking updates, and expressing concerns yourself rather than waiting for other team members to do so. Explain how team members should interact with one another and with you as you take on your management responsibilities for the first time, whether they are formal or informal. Determine the primary communication avenues, such as email or chat servers, so that everyone is aware of what to do in the event of a problem. Check in with your team both collectively and privately to see how they are doing and to promote honest dialogue as a way to resolve issues.

Find logical workflows

Create a workflow process map that shows the roles that each team member performs in finishing a project. You can expect more from each person if you are clear on their specific responsibilities and how they relate to the project as a whole. You may also use it to create a realistic schedule that workers can follow. Managing staff without being familiar with the project process may generate confusion and delays and hinder you from quickly determining the root of any problems that arise.

Tolerant personnel management

Employees are given direction and assistance by the management, but are free to choose their own actions, including directing results.

When there may be several "right answers" and workers are skilled and capable in producing a favorable conclusion in the particular context or company, this approach is often more beneficial for the workforce and may provide superior outcomes.

Make the proper hires

Any organization's success depends on selecting the proper employees. Making the incorrect choice when hiring someone may result in a lot of time and effort being lost that might have been saved by making the proper choice the first time.

But how can you tell whether someone is capable? The best method to find the perfect candidate is to conduct an interview that includes both technical and non-technical questions about their background, objectives, and beliefs as well as questions about your business or sector. This can help you determine if they would be a good addition to your team.

While there is not a secret to finding the right candidates, I have had success by identifying the behaviors that are necessary for the position, interviewing candidates for those behaviors, and including team members who will work closely with the new hire—even if they are not directly on my team—in the interview process.

Remember this advice: Hire slowly and dismiss quickly. If you make a bad hiring decision, try quickly to get rid of them so you can discover the ideal candidate to support the objectives of your team and business.

Let the individual remedy their own error.
There is no need to discredit one of the staff members in order to demonstrate your "genius." It is preferable to write that individual personally and point out their error instead. Talk about the fix and let

them make the correction on their own.

Allowing individuals to heal on their own eliminates the need to publicly humiliate them. Long-term, this will greatly improve their job.

Guard your folks.
You must behave as the impact-absorbing shield. Nobody should be able to direct your team's actions without your permission. Allow others to critique you if they want to, and you will learn what to do inside your organization.

Makes the hope to get familiar with your staff.

You need to at the very least be familiar with your workers' first names. This applies regardless of the size of your business. Additionally, you have to be aware of their hobbies and interests outside of work. It is crucial to get to know your staff members since doing so will help you understand better how they carry out their duties. Making sure that your degree of attention is acceptable can also assist your staff members feel appreciated.

Give your workers particular attention.

The preceding rule is followed by this one. You will be able to treat each employee as an individual after you get to know them. The strategy you use should be determined by the distinct abilities, preferences, and developmental needs of your staff. In order to manage people effectively, you must focus on each person as an individual and adjust your strategy to suit their requirements.

Make receiving feedback ongoing the norm.

Although it is a gift, feedback is not only the responsibility of the sender. It is the responsibility of the management to provide a dependable, secure atmosphere where staff members feel free to voice concerns.

The more room I can provide for that, the better, said Trevor Sutlej, head of enterprise sales at Jabot, "It is very difficult to give candid, direct feedback." They feel more at ease the more you can achieve that type of open feedback system.

Every week at his one-on-one meetings, he purposefully asks for feedback, a practice he credits to his partner, a sales recruiter for six years. He said, "They are simply supposed to be open discussions, back and forth. "I always ask them verbally if they do not fill it out in the Lattice Update."

Do not be hesitant to provide honest feedback; doing so will assist your team develop feedback skills with one another as well as create a more positive work atmosphere than keeping issues bottled up. Asking effective questions, according to Moon, is the key to receiving practical, actionable feedback from a new team.

Because it is too open-ended, the question "Do you think I am a good manager?" is not one that will elicit a thoughtful answer, according to Moon. Ask for input instead on your leadership style's more particular elements, such as how you interact with others or provide information, how you conduct discussions or meetings, and if you give others the chance to feel challenged and inspired.

Create definite objectives.

Establish objectives both individually and as a team to direct your management efforts. Setting objectives at the outset of a project provides you direction as a leader and maintains everyone's attention on how their actions affect a project's or initiative's success. So that you have a record to refer to when evaluating project progress at significant milestones, write down each objective. Talk about the actions that each team member has to take to reach their objectives with your group, and give everyone the chance to ask questions and provide recommendations on how to achieve your team's goals.

Address poor performance right away

Timing is key when it comes to dealing with subpar employee performance. Speak with staff immediately about their poor performance.

By the time you, the manager, learn about it, others have most likely been affected and, in the worst circumstances, the well-being of specific employees is jeopardized. Performance problems may worsen if they are not handled right away, and a low-performer may grow toxic and infect your team and the whole business.

Employees that consistently miss deadlines or do subpar work, act disruptively or hostilely, or lack engagement or motivation are some examples of bad employee performance.

Be sincere and discuss the future. Be honest at all times. Tell them the truth if the project has stopped receiving money and will shortly be abandoned. Do not put people before facts if there are intentions to modify anything; instead, inform everyone beforehand.

Do not remain quiet if there are plans for workforce reductions at the organization. It is better to admit after the fact that the plans did not work out than to blame the individuals up front. Inform them as well if the firm intends to increase everyone's pay. It enhances retention while fostering trust. Not to add that teams with open leadership often have superior cultures.

The staff needs to be informed on what is going on with the business, and it would be best if they did so from you.

Everyone on the team should be paid fairly.

It is not always possible to pay employees the greatest salaries available. There will always be a business that offers more wages and a worker who makes more money. But for employees to feel like they have enough value for you and your business, they need to recognize that their pay for your firm is fair.

I use the following approach to determine if the wage is fair or not: Imagine the day when the corporation makes all pay available to the public. Will I feel embarrassed in front of a teammate? If so, their pay has to be adjusted since it is not high enough.

This is how a wage that is too high works. Is it truly a good idea if someone makes much more money than the team members would anticipate? What if word spreads?

Allege full fault.
You are accountable for everything that occurs as a leader. The only way to determine what needs to be

done inside the team internally is after you have accepted full responsibility for the error.

Whoever was really at fault may not matter to those on the outside, but those who are inside must feel safe and taken care of. The team must have the impression that, even if the mistaken person is eventually fired, it was not done under duress but rather after careful deliberation and internal rationale.

Regard for limits

Do not intrude on your workers' personal time or space. Do not aggressively promote any team building activities. Even without your "let us go today," people would still want to interact outside of the workplace.

Vacation time is revered. If a person on vacation has to be called often, something went wrong.

Even after the employee goes, stay in contact

You may launch a new business, or perhaps a position will become available. Even when someone is no longer employed by you, communication should continue—in certain cases, it should even increase. Try to stay in contact with them since you could need some of them again in the future.

Periodically check in on them to see how things are doing and see if they would want to come back. Someone can be embarrassed to ask you to consider returning since they are dissatisfied with their new employment.

<u>HAPPY READING</u>